JUST YOU AND ME

JUST YOU AND ME

Remarkable Relationships in the Wild

Written by
Jennifer Ward

Illustrated by
Alexander Vidal

Beach Lane Books • New York   London   Toronto   Sydney   New Delhi

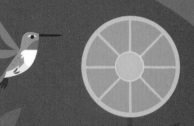

Just you and me.
Just me and you.
We're perfect pairs!
Here's what we do. . . .

Some animals and plants form lifelong partnerships with other animals and plants, a relationship known as *symbiosis*. Then they cooperate and help each other in the most unlikely ways.

I jump inside your sharp-toothed grin
and feast upon the food within.
Your teeth get cleaned. I get a meal.
I'd say that that's a dazzling deal.

When the Nile crocodile needs to have its teeth cleaned, it opens its mouth wide. The Egyptian plover bird hops right in, cleaning the croc's teeth and gums while getting a meal in the deal.

I hold you gently in each claw
and show you off—then you may gnaw
on treats I eat as I explore
the perils on the ocean floor.

The boxer crab carries a stinging anemone in each claw to scare away predators; the anemones then benefit by eating bits of food left over by the crab as it dines.

I am your eyes and look about
for danger lurking on our route.
I can't smell well; I hardly hear.
Your ears are sharp; your nose is clear.

Zebras and ostriches herd together, relying on each other's stronger senses to warn of danger. Ostriches have good eyesight and a high vantage point. Zebras have a great sense of smell and good hearing.

I wear your green among the trees.
You hide me well so no one sees
a hanging sloth that moves quite slow,
as predators lurk far below.

Algae make their home on sloth
fur, turning it green in the process.
This creates camouflage for the sloth,
which helps it to hide from predators.
(Bonus: the algae are also nutritious
and may supplement the sloth's diet!)

I eat your juicy, bright red fruit
and nest within your cactus boot.
And when I wing across the sky,
it's time for cactus seeds to fly!

Tall saguaro cactuses provide shelter and protection for woodpeckers, which create cavity nests inside the cactuses' trunks that harden into "boot" shapes. Woodpeckers eat the saguaro's fruit and then disperse the fruit seeds in their poop, helping to grow new saguaros.

I perch upon your armored back
and pick myself a tasty snack
of little ticks that also ride
upon your dusty rhino hide.

Oxpeckers love to eat ticks—nasty pests that suck the blood from rhinos; the rhinoceros gets its skin cleaned of parasites. Win-win.

I march upon your thorny bark,
protecting you by day and dark
from animals that choose to dine
upon your stems and leaves so fine.

The acacia tree provides sweet food
(sap) and a home for ants, while the
ants guard and fight off herbivore
predators, such as grasshoppers,
that would eat and harm the tree.

I shovel sand and dig a hole;
our safety is my final goal.
Since I can't see, you'll be my eyes
and warn when threats are on the rise.

The pistol shrimp digs a burrow for its home.
Then a goby fish moves in too! The shrimp has
poor vision, but the goby will use its tail to warn
the shrimp when danger is near.

I balance on your back so round,
where tasty bugs are often found.
Eating bugs may seem quite icky.
But if you've got 'em, I'm not picky!

Egrets will ride upon just about anything for a meal.
They're not picky—a zebra, an elephant, a hippopotamus . . .
The egrets get a meal; their travel companions get pest control.

I love to clean. It's in my name.
If you have pests, I'm not to blame!
I'll snack on you from nose to tail;
you'll never have a cleaner scale.

Cleaner wrasses are fish that set up "cleaning stations" in reefs. Eels, sea turtles, and other fish visit these stations to rid themselves of parasites and dead or damaged scales. Visitors get cleaned, and the wrasses get a meal.

I'm the bee, and you're the flower.
Nectar gives me food and power.
I'll spread your pollen plant to plant,
since you are rooted and you can't.

Bees fly from flower to flower, stopping to drink
and gather nectar. Pollen from each flower sticks
to a bee's hairy body each time and gets deposited
on the next flower the bee visits—pollinating the
flower so it may form seeds and new plants.

Just you and me.

Just me and you.

Protecting you is what we'll do.

Earth, you are our only home . . .

from sand to sea, from sky to stone.

Humans cannot survive without the natural resources of Earth, such as water, air, soil, and plants, just to name a few. So we must protect Earth's resources by keeping the environment clean and healthy, harvesting thoughtfully, and practicing conservation. Our survival—and that of the planet—depends on it!

For my daughter, Kelly, who has filled my life with all things wonderful.
And for Andrea—I'm beyond grateful to partner with you on projects.
—J. W.

SOURCES

Engels, T. J. "Cleaner Wrasses Are Vitally Important to the Health of Reef Fish." *Reef Builders* (blog), Oct 23, 2015. https://reefbuilders.com/2015/10/23/cleaner-wrasse/

Landry, C. (2010) Mighty Mutualisms: The Nature of Plant-pollinator Interactions. *Nature Education Knowledge* 3(10):37

Pauli, Jonathan N., Jorge E. Mendoza, Shawn A. Steffan, Cayelan C. Carey, Paul J. Weimer, and M. Zachariah Peery. "A Syndrome of Mutualism Reinforces the Lifestyle of a Sloth." *Royal Society Publishing*, Mar 7, 2014. https://doi.org/10.1098/rspb.2013.3006

Perry, Nicolette. *Symbiosis: Nature in Partnership.* London: Blandford, 1990.

Ramirez, Sam, and Jaclyn Calkins. "Symbiosis in Pistol Shrimp and Goby Fish." Reed College, 2014. https://www.reed.edu/biology/courses/BIO342/2015_syllabus/2014_WEBSITES/sr_jc_website%202/index.html

BEACH LANE BOOKS
An imprint of Simon & Schuster Children's Publishing Division
1230 Avenue of the Americas, New York, New York 10020
Text © 2021 by Jennifer Ward
Illustration © 2021 by Alexander Vidal
Book design by Lauren Rille © 2021 by Simon & Schuster, Inc.
All rights reserved, including the right of reproduction in whole or in part in any form.
BEACH LANE BOOKS and colophon are trademarks of Simon & Schuster, Inc.
For information about special discounts for bulk purchases, please contact Simon & Schuster Special Sales at 1-866-506-1949 or business@simonandschuster.com.
The Simon & Schuster Speakers Bureau can bring authors to your live event. For more information or to book an event, contact the Simon & Schuster Speakers Bureau at 1-866-248-3049 or visit our website at www.simonspeakers.com.
The text for this book was set in Aaux. • The illustrations for this book were rendered digitally. • Manufactured in China • 0621 SCP • First Edition • 10 9 8 7 6 5 4 3 2 1 • Library of Congress Cataloging-in-Publication Data • Names: Ward, Jennifer, 1963– author. | Vidal, Alexander, illustrator. • Title: Just you and me / Jennifer Ward ; illustrated by Alexander Vidal. • Description: New York : Beach Lane Books, [2021] | Audience: Ages 3–8 | Audience: Grades 2–3 | Summary: "A fascinating rhyming exploration of symbiosis: how different animals (and even some plants!) help each other in nature"—Provided by publisher. • Identifiers: LCCN 2020052202 (print) | LCCN 2020052203 (ebook) | ISBN 9781534460980 (hardcover) | ISBN 9781534460997 (ebook) • Subjects: LCSH: Symbiosis—Juvenile literature. • Classification: LCC QH548.W37 2021 (print) | LCC QH548 (ebook) | DDC 577.8/5—dc23 • LC record available at https://lccn.loc.gov/2020052202 • LC ebook record available at https://lccn.loc.gov/2020052203